The Ubiquitous Big

THE UBIQUITOUS BIG

Ian Samuels

For Danielle ..
may all your
juxtapositions
be profound.

Coach House Books

Published with the assistance of the Canada Council for the
Arts and the Ontario Arts Council. We also acknowledge
the financial support of the Government of Ontario
through the Ontario Book Publishing Tax Credit Program
and the Government of Canada through the Book
Publishing Industry Development Program (BPIDP).

NATIONAL LIBRARY OF CANADA CATALOGUING IN PUBLICATION

Samuels, Ian, 1975-
       The Ubiquitous Big / Ian Samuels.

Poems.
ISBN 1-55245-135-6

    I. Title.

PS8587.A3624U34 2004   C811'.54   C2004-900308-9

For T.

ARCANA

They invented the printing press out on the plain
this morning; Constantinople fell in the afternoon.
I suppose they'll discover America tomorrow. What
a lot of running around they do.

– Kenneth Patchen, *The Journal of Albion Moonlight*

No business like ...

There was a giant ponderous on stilted legs,
biding his time till he'd finally outrun those
plastic packages of Brussels sprouts that just
wouldn't die (and over his music you could hear
bombers drop fire in five-foot stanzas).

There was a reservist with a guitar and the way
he spat out the bullets sounded just like a night
on the Delta.

There was a walking jukebox on the West Bank
belting out 'White Christmas' and saying, 'I'm
entertainment, even when Nature fails,' conver-
sation over.

All chemical

The Word looked up at a slumming comet whose tail dragged a dozen mythic astronauts in its wake, old Texans all, who'd spent a thousand years mouthing unborn ballads into the big empty.

The Word catalogued old tenements as it slipped along the paper walls, a red ink snake sinuous around a cool-walled chamber, flickering fork-tongued yearnings over a porcelain rose and a wood-etched manifesto.

The Word wrote itself into a revolutionary thrill-ride over the cliff's edge and was first to split the hairs of an argument on razored stones, the first to hear how friendly the gunships really were.

Whiching

If there's a little truth in truth it's this drop of rain searching for an umbrella, a peyote dream bullet through the skin of a criminal face down in the sage, a cross-boned line in white dust stilling blood on a green-backed gully while the wind cries in a circle and tells stories of how the vanishing bottle choir changed the ave for a wind that turned north to embrace river droplet reflections, call back Maria, scatter through possible worlds to make one dollar a cause.

Discipline

The birds rouged their cheeks and sketched a
courtly bow to the Bentham brothers.

They sang 'Hush Now' with nine-millimetre
percussion backing and echoed strains of a jazz
contagion across the high green valleys of a
country that finally got famous by burning itself
slow over a civil war blaze.

They hit Grenada in formation with the memory
of Saigon etched through lightning in their fore-
brains and picked through the pale stretched
skin of a boy out of the closet down to the
skeleton.

Meat country

The sausage king lounged in a villa, blew smoke rings in the shape of Martha Raye's last dream of Broadway and slipped a waltz under an arch of bologna through a two-inch layer of fat on the cobbles shining a cheap pickup line at the moon.

Somewhere under the town, all the vanished children gathered over the ancient bones of dynamited coolies communion style under a cleaver-wielding stone image of Our Lady of the Primal Rib, proving this was meat country pillaged straight from an emperor's gut.

Oracular

The Latin writ on the priest's severed tongue was
a hymn to:

  smokestacks,
  Maxim guns defending a teacup empire,
  a half-million terminal films of soldiers in step
       (rifles on shoulders and eyes shining on
         a future whose Rockwell paintings and
         nuclear reactors have bottled a limited-
         time offer to rise up
                  up
                      and ...)

Trysting

Frozen paramours curl spoon-fashion in the wreckage of Ultima Thule, a community of walls trading in politic silence where men court their brides through a stone-tap argot and the young conjugate a verbal empire-waisted limelight of spinning cane and suckle at a raw culture of revolving restaurants sovereign over four compass points, their assimilation tied not-yet to Fanon's leg overboard.

Bullish

Product placement behind the explosion of
signs directed a civilization's march into a
random recall of the blood-speckled past,
flanked by faithful shepherding tanks into
unyielding dreams of blasted corpses powdered
under the treads of freedom.

Corporal

The prisoner choked down a chunk of liver and
begged for conquest, swaying one step at a time
away from the whip toward a mind's-eye utopia
of sealskin tires and teardrop-flavoured Jacobin
edicts mixing with salt and a journey home to
scar over the traces of the first time – to achieve
a blur of red into azure and the open road at last.

Hajj

The Word fell in front of a firing squad.

The Word touched the walls of its prison sentence of savannah strewn with T-34 husks, their barrels trained on a forgotten enemy and playing ghost harmonies with the dust storms.

The Word got up and limped east to where a cool new river trickled down, glacial tears from a White Mountain already locked in dreams of Funicello frolics.

The Word stumbled over a corpse face down and dressed to kill in pearls and ermine on a slow journey from a nameless cocktail party of pounding mortars.

Opportunity lands

The bus driver couldn't believe his luck, moving in a fast, aquamarine deep-end Dilbert Dunker experience that had his lungs thanking him.

Somewhere ahead, a sunspot haloed a model-quality twentysomething as she moved into a free loft perking a rich French or Italian blend with a lurcher flouncing behind her through oversized soft cream cushions and artful pasta platters of *Lady and the Tramp* cachet, developing attachments to stereophonic hand-crafted boyfriend facsimiles perched on their left elbows in alpine fashion perking at each other.

Gumption

Captain Industry stripteased a hillside under an infinite cloud Canadarmed in EH-SL on CNN in a single morning's hard-earned mutation.

His house stayed on its back for nine days until its hermetic-chambered mummies packed their bags and climbed into a main-street coin-toss career, hoping eventually to become a prime-time episodic family.

Extinction

The Negro invasion headline's trumpet note hangs on C minor.

It kicks until a harmony inhales the dustbowl pollution and the moneyed blood of a generation of planters runs back to Atlantic where television screens croon 'Begin the Beguine' in ghost signals to five centuries of fish carcass and drowned songlines point to the Door of No Return or Refund policy.

Heroics

Gun at the ready, the Senator watches every shadow and uses caffeine to keep his aim a hundred percent superhuman for taking out the trash.

It's time to hunt around a four-walled life that chokes down against the barrel.

It's time to pulse the moment of truth and separate the enemy from their god-given twitches.

It's time to eat a chalk outline with a bitter pill boxed in with the body count headed for a trick ending. (The hero gets a windup sidekick and a gun, or his girl gets gunned – actual times may vary.)

Arrivals

The gods crawl the last fifty miles of a pilgrimage to Matsuyama where they carve an animal into the soil, its last gesture a quizzical turn of head sideways to contemplate the stalked and now forever unseen prey.

The gods gather for a swill of sake in the last volcanic breath of an island yearning for a descent beneath the waves, away from the demands of cellphones and rat-race lifestyles that tear into its face.

The gods smile at each other with poison-slicked knives secret behind their backs and stir to the rhythm of a Geiger counter's memory of Trinity and the walls coming down.

Symmetry

Most bandits came through the pandemic with a talisman of virgin violation and secured the order of things in a desert made for sacrifices, for the forced removal of every unwanted pound with a fullproof flesh-eating strep diet (no more fads guaranteed just ask our satisfied ...)

They rebuilt culture's perpetual myth mechanism with driver's side airbags and remote keyless entry to the automated murder sweepstakes, a chance to dream Africa as continental playground for the dictator bloating on hijacked riches to pass the savings on to you.

Impact

The wings ignited a global bombardment vision and sent bits of divine spark screaming to street level, where flash captured a Kodak moment's yearning for the death-squad shimmy seared into the whites of their eyes and brought a whipped-cream delicacy sugared by child labour back into style.

Roam

A gang of lost children sat on the highway with a circle of well-to-do vultures explaining their carrion policy.

They dipped toes in a sunlit pool of dust floated from a metric tonne of monarch skeletons flown in on special order; chewed popcorn and looked on at the last great lynching, warm in a torchlit circle, while the wire flashed news of hillsides stripped to a moonscape.

They fingered disposable razors and memories of dynamite chewing through bedrock.

Westphasic

The Word listened for a hint of *The Magnificent Seven* still trapped somewhere in the guts of a robot factory whose cool hands shaped long grass blades with tenderness and churned electric signal code into miles of cool prairie under a cumulus Arch of Triumph.

The Word confronted a siren god with sinews of red and blue light, hands curled around intimate crack of club against bone on a lonely stretch of road.

Balkanized field theory

A dirt track slants down to the riverside chapel
that named Africa the bottom rung where even
the shadows know what lurks overboard:

> knife-scored orbitals,

> a model of revolution-red cells for
> change in the meat aisle,

> rebels on their backs in the grass who
> watch a maze of stars over the wartime
> calcium deposits.

Morning

There was good coffee and fresh rolls steaming just like a kill on the savannah, except with more butter churned up by refugees walking to shore and climbing into thousands of forgotten boats.

The men would take reds in the morning and blues in the evening, would stay blue with the cold, blue men with cold eyes (blue-dyed eyes with gold teeth in their pockets to buy a picket fence and a can of bleach to blend in).

Famine

Dearth: as in a ~ of exquisite hip softer than Soviet currency: as in a ~ designed to make your porn panoptic: as in a ~ on military field of painted bodies traced in toxic dance: as in a ~ of hyperreal forty-fives built around one Word: as in a ~ing of water political in how it fails to soothe: as how to ~ that platonic sceptre in a completely unracialized fashion: as in a ~ thereof.

PERSONALITY

The material contained in this text has been completely revised and modernized with respect to the science (theory) and the art of cosmetology.

– Pearl C. Ware, *The Marvel Textbook of Cosmetology*

This is a disappearance manual for elimination, a girl transforming herself with a tumour, a golden scent of incense hanging over the gridlocked Real, a growing physical language, a literature composed only for living friends, a need to please all, a new way to live, a pleasing breath odour and a strained sleep with abdomen curving to rib cage, aching with frustrated fluencies.

Beautiful science is patterned to follow its owners, so be yourself: be pleasant, be candid, be a saviour for those whose lives are trapped in a circle of living rooms cramped with the party favours of forgotten years. Be a longing patriot and balance your serenity with occasional pirouettes in the living room, but avoid the regular model of artless precision and stay straight at all costs, even should it mean a long swallow of cordial. Reach out to your father, and remember no one ever fell off the edge of sanity from a wheelchair in a retirement home. Soft-shoe to your customers' talk and obey the public will faithfully. This is it, the War on Tastelessness, a time to match wits with your competitors any chance you get. Grooming is an art, so grill yourself a piece of rat and extend your left foot into a pool of liquefied rock candy like distilled childhood. Demand your very own glimpse of the birth of atomic power.

Your broken serenity reveals a taste for fresh almandine poisons, a way to celebrate the individuality of 'you.' Chant your movements into a mechanized temporal lobe, and cherish your good reputation while you choke on pesticidal fairy dust. People learn the value of lotion during a locust attack. Prune politics and the conversation blooms: you won't use anything ugly to determine your cosmetic personality and map it onto your eyebrow with a sharp, thin pencil.

Pay attention as secret voices show you the proper way to pick a brush off the floor or grip a knife handle: parade your instep and arches correctly, never curve your spine. Slide back, fix your address on a lively art deco stretch, and enjoy thinking outside the box but don't offend your patron. Empty your work of doubt and wield your comb like a sword to cut your way free from the purgatory of shuffling gaits.

You've learned to spot a low-heeled anger in the smooth uniforms and robotic joy of your customers; this means They* are waiting to feed you into an organ harvester.

*They: the press in Paris, the peaceful Parisienne, the well-manicured intellectual whose will to live is a plastic-fanged thing trapped in an attic and pining to be part of your personal life, to set your city in migration from the summer heat, to make your complexion into property, your lumpy anxieties draped in sackcloth and stalking you with ill intent.

The harrow carves an *h* with knives on automatic into your hunger for chocolate ice cream with rainbow sprinkles. You can have your vital Italy or live in Essex with the repressed and badly shaved pensioners, watching them squirm. You've noticed the trace images on your eyelids swirl into an apocalyptic glow, an incandescent cosmos a breath away from collapse.

Cosmetologists can be free from the flesh dilemma if they keep thinking Truth, so work on your flexibility and get a quart of the viscous pale fluid we manufactured to balance sex and art, confident the chord struck by your minor voice would consign the Dark Continent to a Can-Do wasteland. Everywhere, the android plan will soon deliver evolution and demand betrayal, so learn to choose your sense of humour and exile your foreign accent if you still have one.

If you find yourself on a bridge in Moscow waiting for a microfilm, use these moments to count the possible routes between the chairs in your salon. Deep down, you will feel a need to contribute to the public health, welfare and safety of the community, so consider the beauty of marbled steaks and falling trees. Consider becoming and speaking your jealousy. Consider that what seems improper at certain intervals and between certain teeth – say, the soft carcass of a misty country known only in songs or the names of films, a *Casablanca* or *Brazil* – actually came to you to suppress a colour riot and convince you of the simple fact that capital is everywhere, just like meat. Confine the spreading profane with self-disciplinary confidence in your complexion: condition your body and mind with good emotions, clean and confident with a special cereal toy to conceal the simple terror that infects every second. Buy business cards that make the world notice with holographic display; bend to the right and make sure your karmic centre is working. (Also make sure you know what 'karmic' means.)

In a flickering confession, the universe will possess your television and call you a product of sadistic factory noise. Still, you can make a living on the edge of the spaghetti western desert where a boys' underground nation was once greased and thrown to the MGM lion. Be beauty, antiseptic but possible, be liveliness, be loyal to your employer, manager, school and associates. Beautify your heart murmur: become quality, become yourself, use the electrode science, believe your business *can't* construct a sluggish circulation. Belong in the confusion of data, bend gracefully to shoulder your burdens and blacken the air with iconic dreams of flawlessness.

Boarded by inspectors, your ship listing into an oil-painted wave, branch into loud living and breathe the five-hundred-year traces of invisible vessels. At table while your eye spills brown water, a coded signal can back your business instincts with firepower – but a bad reception can stain even the most brilliant cosmetologist, so circulate your ideals in the wake of missile explosions and stay balanced through your centre in a display fit for the silvered screen.

An efficient mind means a radioactive glory for the salon: your memories will monopolize knowledge and the common throat, put out the tongue at its bleeding root, conquer a pile of dead canines to the music of nails on a counter-top. Your flowers should be test pattern-toned, keeping the average immigrant pliable for manual or voice operation while genetic science faithfully imports a dance of grief into your potatoes.

It's cosmetology in action, scattering your wishes by aerosol spray. Your couture dispenses with the Reds and cultivates blue voices growing in a green pattern, calming the callous-thumbed video arcade lifers stewing in their drowsy afternoon envy of the inner circle. Enlist your city's water supply in strong measures against the depression of the homeless.

Be a national example of the soft instep and live a politics of deathless gloss with a roundabout to enlightenment just the next side of a traffic light in Crete, where the women are stocky and prize honesty. This is an important time: only you can keep the East wrapped in ramshackle bazaars, keep the arteries of finance clean.

If you groom your palace carefully, your every intention will be both plain and pure. Apply the same approach to cold-waving. Your appearance is as important as your skills, but it won't be enough to save the good works reflected piecemeal in the edifices of falling towers unless you void your meals at regular times and sleep under a sand dune where filing clerks once groped through papered stacks of madness and learned to love the thought regulations that kept their profession moving into a tale of green (gables or berets). The manual reminds us how important a plunge into volcanic steam can be for long-term health, remarking that all women seem to choose the hot regions.

Listener, listen to her, listen here: live long, live loud above the stain of sleep and lounge by the pool, pretending it's the kind of sea your navy might tame with offerings of oil and sailors' corpses. Swallow the sparkle of a charm bracelet while you measure a peasant woman's life against the breadth of a chaise.

Remember, it's not ideas but people that obey, and every sale will line your teeth with the silvered flavour of discoloured lovers.

Sensible children befriend ex-Soviet guns smoothed by their passage from hand to hand, out where vertigo seizes the slick inner surface of a leg muscle and your stomach clenches into a pentacle of malice. You must never be inside, at least not enough to offend any normal habits. Develop a personal approach to the cityscape, a diet of good meat and duty. Widen your world as you spy the world's final sex act trapped in a blue note, sealing the casket of a Scarlett idol and lighting her rapture.

Clean your nails while cocaine leaves the maize stillborn in its shadow. Poised to escape Necessity, your problem skin is on its way to a European phase, itching with speech. Sanity never sold a style – that's the kind of thinking that gets professionals eaten by pulp-novel Ashanti (remember the exorcists who thought for us until they found the hellmouths right on our threshold). Purchase a neureality, come as a penitent to voice your joy; come to love your universe's being.

Name your accessories Guy, Sandra, Edna and so forth. Pass on the sort of neon knowledge one might find on a dead-end street at the heart of an urban sprawl: a few friendships are no match for the comfort of envy, of watching a woman (but only a woman) with a butcher knife in your hand. Note the whiteness of teeth, the instinctive brush of hand against face. Effectiveness is the first word in treatment, teasing your brain into a back-stem reverse curl while the emoticons in your e-mail stage a pseudo-Romance revolution.

A duel at dawn (Greenwich Mean) over a fine-textured skin, timed precisely by the wristwatch of a passing gentleman so each parry and riposte falls precisely in the first or last quarter of a single second, generates a regular rhythm to induce adequate sleep in the object. You must have a proper diet and patrons to admire you, to ask how you took five and three-quarter seconds to transform a paste-board peace into a papier-mâché war, making both of them look glamorous and somehow erasing the memory of Amritsar, all without shuffling your feet, all while walking with a precise angle to your parasol, avoiding bad breath and body odour and gaudy jewellery and the long still stares of the ungrateful.

Cowherds look up as psychic lines transform the voice of their beloved, as their bosses pace by with cocked rifles singing songs about the dairy plague that shake your clam and make you vow to be comatose – particularly after you see a retouched shot of the young families you're eating, once so lucid and defiant. How never to get lost in this stolen valley: let hygienic emotions adjust your voice while you turn your hair into a spun-gold fortune and wait for the impresarios to find you. Eventually you'll come across a broke-down commune catering to everyone, its RCA Victor still on the blink, still serving a gilded mistress.

Education learns to deafen the ear and advertising gives a position against the Native, an exposure to a half-remembered Trinity cleansing your acne with fragments of African voice bleeding through the palm oil. A graceful anemic turns, points, bends to apply a well-balanced ethics now appraised at four points above the mean, the arc-en-ciel breeding stable personality in sober shoes (important to arch correctly).

Are your studies done? Now practice your cosmetology in a public venue, arguing with the ants while their mouths strip you to a tune written in lowercase letters leaving all that holds up your personal life, and act rigid, but only when there's someone in earshot. Advise an extrovert to burn her patron's hair down to the scalp and adjust to being almost important, an acute sensation in the nerve bundle, an actress in video romps through a vista of fatal femmes, acid visions inspired by the latest longing for heaths and able to stomach welcoming committees of virtually any shape, even to become a lonely commentary on the prompt self-destruction of society without school prayer, or a cut of the brittle eighties in a city throwing curtain of perpetual predawn over the land, in a civilization built on shared love of glossolalia, a cushion for unexpected landings.

THE UBIQUITOUS BIG

In Italy, for thirty years under the Borgias they had warfare, terror, murder and bloodshed, but they produced Michelangelo, Leonardo da Vinci and the Renaissance. In Switzerland, they had brotherly love, they had five hundred years of democracy and peace – and what did they produce? The cuckoo clock.

– Orson Welles, *The Third Man*

A bitter world

Ammunition goes with being together when you look around the world. I'd like to get back to why you're bitter, but first I want to kiss the front fender's polish, to know why the guns liked it. I didn't say 'little lady,' I said it's a bitter world, I said it looks like we could go places but it's too far to get out of the house – I don't think and you take so long to say what you want.

Made for mauling

A touch of class, sure, but I'm really a hound and I was made for mauling. In case you don't know, my appetite depends on who's doin' the do. You know about scenery and marked cards, but I don't know how far to let this game go. You're an hourglass looker in a thousand saddles and that's why I like talking about horses, making sure to capture some of that speed for an oil-painted gloss. You've got the hips that really make the bayou work and the next hand's hanging on what you can do with them and a lot *you're* doing. All right, PLEASE.

Nothing but the buck

I'd have chewed through any side of meat you handed me, if I'd only been raised on a ranch. It suddenly hit you in one of those dives that you'd never been to the Big Apple and this sure as hell wasn't it – where was the skyline and the life-or-death battles over dancing? You'd be surprised: in thirty years, the wide prairie told anyone who didn't know that love is first and second is nobody, it's this town making its own dawn and I'm *it*, the bastard your speech writers have been dreaming of, so you ought to eat your oysters. How does a gumshoe in a cheap brown suit know what communism is? It's really about whether you'd like to buy a tie or defenestrate every man you ever met, and maybe they all had it coming. Haven't I been murdered before? You would never have thought of me as a no-good tax adjuster or census-taking rat if I didn't have a pair of smooth black gloves in my apartment. In the end, there's nothing but the buck, the smeared blue emblem of a man who hates to think off the Bridge (that's Kensington, Brooklyn or Golden Gate), who took five pictures that came into focus when they hit the crick bed. I'll bet that's when he saw how the bar could be a mecca – there's nothing like a cornfield to tell you how to waltz through the sound of your own jokes, to be the wittiest, finest of the species, the very thing, the heart of a scene.

Mirror phantom

It's not lavish, but I still call it home and change
the fleas. This comforter's for girls who don't
have any wallets to make, but don't tell them,
honey: I like the way I learned Spanish and I like
this drawn-out bottled euphoria. My conscience
says, 'It's your rock bottom now, just put your
lips together and blow until you can't sink any
lower' – that's how I know this rotten-toothed
mirror phantom can't possibly be me. The sign
outside says 'fresh,' just like how the Feds gut a
warehouse before it occurs to them that, oh,
maybe the place looks lived in. Yeah, blow up
the dump and stop calling me; it's a great hotel
but don't claim that roach-ridden cot was all I
liked about you.

The hacienda

A cup of coffee, that's what a man needs. An apple, a place I can feel, a growth that looks like chicken. Dinner with the family lasted seven months, but why not? In the bonds of matrimony that's how the Feds weigh cellophane off a cigarette pack. They tell the core stuck between my teeth how it's a crummy finger joint, but a nickel gets a piece of the 'haves' and a drink keeps murder heavy on my soul until the bungalow sags right to its floorboards. How's the chicken cacciatore, you ask? A little sore since you torched it with the cooking sherry, but Mom tasted kind of like old clubhouse – that's why the only hotel in town's got a dining room now, quite the hacienda I hear, plenty of class. Hey, waitress, this steak is still. My guilt said, 'Don't buy more ice than I could use at the bar or I'll open your gut for the rats in the wall.' That girl had it in for me, but I can't say her two husbands were turnips when we were going to the Antlers and you bet it's swell how they try to live on in the pit of her stomach.

Hundred-to-one omelette

There's a carload of hats in it for a private detective who gets a third-rate joint on Fourth, for all that getting hitched doesn't always look so chivalrous to strangers. What am I, a bowl of sand? I'll stake you to any tense and walk out. I had asked your husband for money but it's as if two people got dead just trying to find better quince. 'Let me go dispose of the weak,' said my brass knuckle, 'or do you want to keep your life?' Doesn't it bother you that the door's still open and I've been gone for years? I can't help remembering the night a thousand reels of gangster film fell like a burning float onto First Street. So many chances, but what if my four months' worth of big ideas come up with small fruit, a peeled tangerine? After all, I've got a nice build but I'm the kind of mug people trip over in the parking lot. Listen, if being tossed headfirst from a window into a rainbow-brite morning isn't on the menu, then what's to interest me? It costs one more zeppelin crash for two to duet, one more hole in the pavement, and that's why you have to know the law. This bite is for the last time I looked at you and when I learned to cook my first hundred-to-one omelette – you know very well who'd like those odds, but it's still likely to be fatal. This bite is your life summed up in a minute, in the trunk of an Oldsmobile, in a rotten tryst.

Kick the working day

It's time for a one-off at the neck so stick with me, kid, and live twice as much as I seem to in the dreams where I think it's snooks on all women, or maybe just on you. We still haven't got a diamond, but people like us, don't they? A gumshoe lives for beatings 'cause he has a sense it's the only good thing for shysters and two-bit thugs who live without Swiss watches. Somehow I'd wind up seeing the street, you know how much I stuck in there with stardust in my gut. 'Look in your hats,' they all say, the ones who know about the world I despise, that place where no one's got to do the lindy hop. Ain't much time for conversation and I couldn't begin to kill people and that's why I chant, to keep strong under any name the Ouija board could give me. This caper'll work unless we want to hold hands; I'm the used, I know it, but that's another thing that happens to cellophane. Tell the captain we'll kick the working day; that's why he wrapped a piano around his girl – he didn't want to lose, to let her live. Listen to a flat-foot when you're talking about blues murder and don't look down.

Shoot the next man

I may be a hopped-up show-off but I know until you're sick for the hammer like a blackmailer, you can either pay the captain off or set up a hit. Did you ever want to even up a killing? Never stay for the shot, never get off on it: you're here to kill a man, kill him now, and I'm already leading the lunatics to the gas station. Next time you're penniless you can call stage but don't be a Moses sucker that gets knocked off. There's a corpse in all the best buzzwords, so use them if you want any scratch – that's how to deal with your secret, to bury a dead hero and shoot the next man that says 'when.' Always carry your own key until the tune loses track of you.

To kiss a thief

I made my way around a cocktail lounge like a *live* coward, found where they kept the liquor and the buttons and the rusty pistols. They said, 'Careful not to pass out, citizen,' but my crime was right next door going rotten green and grey and drawing flies, so now I run stings out of skyscrapers, I'm feeling low enough. Downing a bourbon this early didn't trouble my memory of false arrests: that's how my few brains got food value. Miss, I distrust people who forget too fast. The gas goes in like fresh air but, as the saying goes, don't look at a funeral parlour waiting for the wedding to begin. A mime's about to explain why everybody wants lunch money for a good memory of that special someone who got an early start when wormwood crept into his arteries. The murder would've happened anyway and the smell still would've hung on me. I finished your sewage for you so you could be the one to kiss a thief; I wouldn't stand for sitting around. That smooch was a piece of the same old collar, darling, and it only takes a little laundering to love such a locked-up twist of fate. That's why I run bourbon straight to where guys have a thousand more ways of making suckers.

Post-murder glow

Our neighbour looks as though a job keeping pace with the rest of the world through only one eye and spitting crimson markers out the other hasn't exactly watered his lawn, but whoever said it was for his own good added, 'You've got a piece of the newspaper and your readers are smart,' so here's to the cargo of guns that got the suckers moving when the afternoon faded into a sniper's dusk. The thing to do is sit and be trusting when he tells you it's better to forget tomorrow or the locals won't have nothing to use and you can be sure they'll want to feel complete, so we can't run out of water again. If you want to pull outta this burg, I'd start drinking bourbon and leave this city steaming – but where would it get me if my last word means whatever you just said? You were smart falling into a certain routine, a chain link leading to the other shore. It'd be a different game if the little kid in you was really a tramp's post-murder glow, but isn't that ahead of today's agenda? We were supposed to do anything but burn a beautiful yacht.

Canary

Now look, buster, you've been caught on film just as if you lived for being picked up by a bimbo. In this day and age I'd bump myself off once the lindy hop got monotonous, but then burglars don't always work at night. I'll give you a murderer but only because you're special – so tell me, canary, what do you do for cheap flashy poison when a whole cathedral gets crooked? I'd never have figured you to depend on girls named Lucy, but a detective's got to play all the roles, right? I'll die protesting your innocence, but what's different is that when your body comes through the skylight impaled on a moonbeam, all anyone will think is 'We'll find his cardigan and get some scratch.' Truth is, everybody wants to be a face.

Left-handed slugger

The second stiff was an unknown and his death wasn't even my doing, it's just what happened when I got mixed up with a nobody's bedsores. I decided to take the money and stick it all up the new holes I'd just opened in gods and men, to say, 'I'm booking, gotta draw the line somewheres even if you're a guy with no wheels.' I caught a whisper that a gumshoe might tapdance on my head with a lead pipe. Here on second base it's just you and me – left my partner back at the haberdashery so maybe I could go home and figure how honeysuckle can be like murder. I like to jump on the apple crates in 4/4 time, but I thought he'd be happier with the Bartok; I'm afraid to guess, now. Did I want to get even, walk in and hit him straight on into the sixteenth century? In this racket there's nothing for a left-handed slugger unless it's a smart-cracking dame who doesn't care what kind of a dish she is. I know this hideout like I've known you, ever since you were crumpled on my stoop in cast-off clothes. Yeah, that's the sugar and this is the look, sharp like all your dresses. I don't win, I just lose more slowly, so if the flies come round it's all the same to me. Sometimes murder can smell like a real lady, today, for instance, as I get my piece of the Tolosa Gold. See, there's the captain – he never told me he was dead, but I guess he didn't know how he'd make out with three strikes against.

In the gravy

I saw some kind of bug-shaped flying machine,
the unknown killer built one that uses buttered
cats on a loaded crane. On a bourbon run I
moved over and saw a face partial to blondes
who didn't figure in a single horrible radio serial.
How many bodies does it take to remind you
that even the sixty-cent special is simpler than
going insane? There's something about crime
that looks blue, and later it's always: 'Stop calling
her a dame in that tent you're wearing and get
that leopard skin off!' When you're planning an
escape to the countryside, you can't leave no one
in the gravy. Even a fake crime is about pursuit
of happiness from the sidewalk where I was
shot, so now it's time to say 'Don't hold your
nose in other people's underworlds' and mean it.
I recognize the mysterious use of looking back-
ward, it's the way to achieve perfect play and the
way to win, but if there's anything I don't like it's
seeing a trail of fallen red flares along the street.
'Thou shalt not kill' is through wasting Holly-
wood's film till the gangsters circle around again.
To be against two laws is to know that a guy
made up from pictures of boys half-covered by
soil and looking glassy into the camera would
see us as a sour geek feast of nails brought up to
spit out. Such a man came out our way, walking
under the most fearful cloud of rust in all the
world, and that's why the gumshoes got me – but
if the sun gets through the vapours there's a way
to rebuild the shiny robot that pours coffee for
mister in the kitchen of the future, and that's

what I heard my girl pursue. What's the use of looking? Well, whenever I saw one of those flat-foots I thought, 'Why can't a pretty girl grift with *my* squad?' Work off the place like scraping off your shell – wouldn't it be fun to agree to almost anything in a clip joint? I'll try to pick you off tomorrow, but I'll have to grab your neck for the biblical injunction so consider getting yourself a closetful of clothes and a suit to remember.

Big time crook

The joint's just a little homey, but maybe my inner small-time crook will tell me all about women and how some are the 'ain't' type that makes it all right to hate. My fingernails scraped the walls clean of accusing eyes and curved legs but I want them there now. I know a nice guy who blew up right in this book, just so I wouldn't be born dumb. You're a good reminder about whatever I did but I bet you'll be the one to smart with the left hook, what woman hasn't? I used a gun for the couple in room 24, I did it for you, didn't dream it in a dream either, and now I can give you a dog-eat-dog cocktail party again. I finally got to the top for a piece of fudge, so the future starts right now. A girl whose first engagement ring poisoned a goldfish is good enough for me – for a long time we'll have a happy, normal home, long as I have a great big dollar sign where my guts churn. I don't care *what* I have but I know you like how I try not to find out. I'm a big-time crook, I'm in the big game in a nutshell and in brief, the income tax goes to a faith healer who knows how to dress up. With me you'd be a man, sister, but I like how most women have a heart.

Mouse

'A nice guy,' you'd say and he'd say, 'What of it? I
want your stash, your chicken-shaped growth,
your aluminum-sided piece of the world, so set
it up or go under. Hey, Mouse! Go out and buy
me a pack of butts!' I don't feel sorry even for a
tick when the little goon goes running and the
boss says, 'Hey, rack the balls!' and we all know
what he *really* means. Poor Mouse.

Tips from the kitty

Sell out your own mother if she's got any scratch on her, then sit tight: you're smart enough to know when some guys are born to embezzle and they're stupid enough to get caught taking bribes. I want the best of everything, but this is the bottom of the barrel. Getting way up high to sell makes the game work, even with chimps. You're out tonight – tonight's where you want tips from the kitty, want what she's got but the diamond went to a man who was just like she was, a patchwork of wounds. Anyway, with no holds barred you could have a cardboard box mansion where it's always balmy. I didn't care for that nun, only she might knock you down and take your cash, shell it out to the big players. If you work in a malt shop you're going to see her, a piece of her that'll haunt all your broken rear-view mirrors.

Inhuman positions

Seems a bit harsh, but to someone in my profession (I'm a quack) she must have been quite given to seeing aliens, hearing their singsong talk, even eating at their restaurants, choking down a plate of live worms, going back with them to their Sinatra-plastered lairs and discovering inhuman positions. Well, for once, *do* something about that rotten flatfoot – I'm going to think about you as you used to be, big with an 'I' voice back when your fist was running this town; that's the picture of you that still shines, foot planted on a bloody-mouthed gumshoe. So I'm no good, which is to say I'm the one who left you with a case of gangrene years ago when you were decent to me and all the cheap crooks were in the joint, eating spears of asparagus. As you know, I've already been kicked but if you still want to carry a grudge at least take it out with a cudgel on someone who can't swing back.

Friendship

To argue a criminal to death, you must first be
able to take off my tie and trip into a rainstorm
singing with every slice of lung you've got left.
Turns out all the crooks are here, so what's the
matter? Don't *what*? Forget it: that was the walk
of a man who'd flinch when I bit a steak as if it
were his juicy haunch I was sucking the gristle
from. Well, maybe it was. Whichever way you
turn, the crowd's still wondering if I'll hang a
Picasso: wouldn't you just *die*? If I had to guess,
we were married once and you've come home
before. I was here when the captain's fingers
discovered free will and struck up a friendship
with his eyeballs, you'd hardly believe it, howl-
ing through your dinner. After that I try not to
boil any water when I think about your footsteps
on the porch.

Off-Broadway

Is there a chance there're too many flashbulbs?
When a murderer is caught he usually picks up
any city laws he can find and throws them at
anyone he can recognize. I just drove in the
other direction – after all, I'm a little off-
Broadway, which proves I'm liberal enough to
bury stiffs in my garden and further my interest
in horticulture. Don't find the dawn, how I
detest the dawn, the grass looks like a dead man
who clung to me sobbing, 'I didn't! I didn't!' Go
to China if you don't like my manners – that's
where your next heist should go wrong and get
you executed. I'm good at popping the cork but
I guess you don't remember me or the rusty guns
around this swamp. I'm the only guy who didn't
get out of the racket, it's hard to go out and eat or
hear my own footsteps in the house. Remember,
I am what you haven't got and I don't like your
manna. I don't mind if you bite before I've gotten
ready; in my mind I'm already walking down the
aisle and selling taste sensations if the vintage is
right. The captain's still convinced you must be
just a bad habit, and it comes over me that it's
back to slinging hash and joe if I've been left out,
that's why a lot of weddings have quite unmade
my mind. We'll be a mixture of Park Avenue and
Colonel Mustard. Okay, I never was pretty but I
did grieve over a hacksaw and you in a smock
sentence; some sounds are too crazy by far. So
help me, I couldn't have left my pals roasting on
spits in the long winter evening, I couldn't be
the man that sticks out a foot to slink into a

drugstore and suddenly finds super service. 'Piss on it,' I tell the judge, 'and as for the things you don't hear, that's life and it'll keep playing on the edge of your eardrum.'

Constitutional

A man with a dollar runs out of places to hide from his imagined murders, and there's always a gumshoe ten paces back sloughing off his green rotted flesh on the stool pigeons. I still won't believe that alligators have the right to pass verdict and that has caused me more trouble than I'm worth. I caught the clap, that was my second mistake, but she was the best thing I ever saw outside of a cash register. I know the river personally and I'm convinced my whole life is there even though my wife claimed there was too little water to wash away my family. There are pictures of the captain wandering blind and bloody on First Street that make men think I'm a constitutional liar, that I never really put a hole in him. If you're looking to get married or to try and make a living, understand that I'm still climbing out the window. Nice how his throat was closed, I'm sorry not to have wanted to buy his corpse for a dollar and wash off the dirt and grime. Money isn't dirty, that's what was wrong with last night. You came in with apologies for your mother who wouldn't let you talk about getting scratch and didn't like crooks who wrestle in the semi-finals. She wanted to hook you too when she found you covered in sand, as though you'd just sacrificed yourself in the desert.

Duck and cover

The heist I believed in doesn't stand for laughing at suspenders and it can't win a ball game. You got a coin? Heads I go, feeling that if you step on a kitten I didn't rate a mad frenzy stinging a man's head for a pair of shoes. Thus may we learn about art, the only remaining component of landfills. I'm no masterpiece, I know five men in brown are about to kill me again and I'll drill any bastard who shoots me with my own apologies. I'm running for the beach, so be there; it's the last time I'll see the world of my friends before they learn to duck and cover. Were you cheated in church by someone you loved? The aroma always comes along before you wake, comes at you a second time while you're copping a plea. It's always brothers who can feel the way a crook makes you sick in a corner – but I still don't have the davenport and I didn't know how quiet you'd be, so do what's best for yourself unless you want me to go back to the thugs. That's why you don't care about chewing your omelette – it's not immoral enough to do anyone in.

Misinformed

I know every day a man can eat a piece of puff
fish, put his chest out and strut, chicken-wise.
You know why you're following us and I know
why you hide yourself: that's how you get away
with murder. That's what gives you the right to
go round killing people whenever you go to
Malibu. I slipped back to the good old days
when the old grew older. You'll discover that a
guy in a white suit with red hair, spit-shined
sport shoes and gold rings on his hands tramples
on harmonicas and trades in baseball bats. I
need guns the way other boys need switchblades
or need to tell you when their growths become
well done. The captain's helping every man hang
him by a foot; he's changed through being
buried and now he's no fool. Everybody wants to
relieve an old friend of his left pinky, or maybe
stare at his meatballs. I don't pray to know how
many times it hurts to be tricked. I'll bet you feel
all dead inside, but even if I had become a
zombie I never met one I liked. If you were used
to living I was misinformed; I'll never be so
stupid again, and I'll do what I can to leave your
friend alive because I'm taller than him, or
because you've been rich and I've been lied to.
The captain put twelve shell casings in the earth
in the middle of the day, but it's early yet. In the
morning, well, we'll know more and a politico's
naked ugliness won't be a jolt to our pride, to my
reputation as a killer; another gumshoe just
crawled out of a ditch and knew damn well what
was true.

The ninth inning

Where we're going, they know how to deliver, they know people who know people and they know that I know who's hitting me and I know you were too small in that moment to lay your hands on me so let me give you a cigarette. This morning's good enough to like jive. Me, I'm like that guy who got done for a dozen hard-boiled eggs and a lug wrench. I've met a man to change my name, a man who wears a belt. I came here to meet the cops, no matter if the hoodlums get men who wear suspenders, but my spleen kept wondering, 'Where's the money?' You always have to have more so I think someone's taken my face again and I'm sure my head will do for the rest of the ninth inning. You can't go, there's no time at all, you're not crooks and you know this is a feasible heart-to-heart. It would be horrible enough lying in a pile of marked cards after the shock of my life, but the worst part would be the dogs chewing at my leg. Chief among them who didn't have, you got the worst of American manhood on the water and then, illegal or no, told them the story of our front fender.

The oasis

We fell out at times and sometimes I was out of line so you'd get your own gun. That's what got you the part. The only person left in this world is playing me with an Escherized deck but believe me, rich is prettier. Let's just say I don't know much about sewers where there's not a decent rat. A better friend woulda grabbed you by the smoke, but I see you so little and it was good to see you get staked where there weren't any blues and still love the executioner. I've done a lot that stinks, but ain't it funny how the swamp took justice into its own teeth? I'm sorry, I've forgotten your thought. That's the trouble with you: the coin always rolls under the day and winds up just where my hand won't ever find it. I loved the middle of the desert until the next man came slouching along with his own severed hand in tow. Could be it's the ride, the three cigarettes or the water, but I'm in a world that's already dead and I'm curled up at the oasis, allergic to the machine-gun wedding. If you want me to talk about the bird in your skull, ask for the story of my throat: how this time, it opens up so I can die in bed. It was very easy to hit Laguna, but what happens if they leave us to live in Peru? Tails, I'll finish them to a man.

Rondo

My victims are all such wonderful people. They hold that over me and throw my best deck of cards in the lake. I'd like to see the spars in my stomach, to say the lost times could have taken me anywhere. Sure I was trouble, trying to crawl out, but I didn't know that I'd turn my other cheek up and find it cut. I wasn't playing for you while you went to pick out a heater. 'We're only asking you to wear belts,' I've lied. 'To hell with the book, Captain! What kind of world is it if I can't like what I like?' I sure never thought his men would get around to me. Who knows? I might have lived a whole life nailed up in a house with a nice little pile of assorted journalist fingers. With a paintbrush I'd shuffle, with guns I'd rondo and hear women cry. I'll only come ashore when it's time to cut the cards. Have to watch out, some night the gumshoes might shave my percentile. I'll know if you're the writer, but for the first twenty minutes what's on your mind? As if your subconscious gave up on your teeth, kicked them down your picket-fenced memories.

Personality neckware

There's a field of psychic treatment for a gal who hit the hard times holding me up. A long time ago, you could drop a policeman and sell his uniform for a song. I was ahead of the game but I didn't like being still when it was time for the big angel, when I lost the answers that made me the wisest and anybody else could play my bright royal flush around the walls of my life at a bargain price. You're gonna have fun in silent pictures before your face mimes a broken-down piece of machinery. I'm no worse than you so who cares if you like pearls – don't dames like you wait for a complete line of personality neckware and end up in the river, excited about something I gave out just to feel cheap, and aren't you two feet taller? From now on I'm going funny, that way you've got no way out. Used to get to me that you were that girl, the one to go for slummers. To find a gun makes me blind to how my left hand just killed the doctor, but if I'd wanted to know how little time I had, I'd have taken a jump.

Romance

We're holed up on a disputed borderline, suckers
for a terrain where a minor key can make you a
mill hand. I couldn't get in accidents, the road
curved but I found some good tarmac when I
heard you'd have a place to iron my money.
You're a simple twenty million even though I still
look like I was born in a bag and the bag's been
through quite enough. When they say, 'Any
happy money on you?' – that's when I break. I
didn't always hate 'new car smell,' but inside a
hundred children I can cram only as much
happiness as a vertical cut and my blood was still
dripping and I was feeding Thursday's flowerbed.
Tonight, before you go, admit that what I did for
you was die, I died like crooks who are to die for
and it was the *stuff*. You liked my deathbed small
and I knew lying there would please you. I love
feet, burning hamburger and coffin hotels even if
the few first hours are terrible. I'm trying to hit
forty million but I'm going to be framed by
whoever sent you up. Got a hit, gonna make me
feel happy, grow to a point? Yeah, money, that's
why I have a secretary who looks starved enough
to pay back a little green. I truly had nothing to
do when I was a 'him' long enough for 'him' to get
home. It was about then I went honest and the
dishonest was out a hundred dollars. Money's
nice but I asked for a piece of dog instead, for a
slice of ballpark. Two things I don't know about
you: why I turned my back when I went out to
the garage to wax my Toronado, and why your
hamsters ate their way into last year's newsprint.

I was always in a prison when your mother felt the world tip everything she owned into an open drawer. You never saw the hole I was buried in, but take it from me, you just don't leave me around people when I'm worth this much, so keep my fingerbones to yourself. I admired how your language made it plain that every extra buck has a last year, but *this* year I'm finally getting in. My ethered gag tasted just like you! I didn't hate you like a wife, so why'd we shred the money? You know what my mother-in-law said that night? 'I can't bear to think how easy every window breaks.' Not to get sticky about it, but my travel papers are crawling with flies and my no-good friends are better off dead. Would it be possible in our brief time to press my pants? That would sure be romance to me.

Acknowledgements

Thanks first of all to my family – Jerry, Sylvia and Vaughn Samuels and Shereen Tuomi – for all their unstinting support and friendship. Many thanks also to Nicole Markotic, whose advice and guidance was crucial to the writing of this book, and to Jay MillAr, Alana Wilcox and Jason McBride at Coach House Books for all their wonderful work in making it happen. For their advice, influence and encouragement I would like to thank Louis Cabri, Darren Wershler-Henry, derek beaulieu and especially my good friend Jonathon Wilcke. Thanks also to Fred Wah, Anne Green, Shanne Matthews, Ellen Busby, Richard Horvath, Tony Snow, rob mclennan, Ashok Mathur, Jason Christie, Andre Rodriguez, Kerry Clarke, Sonya Scott, Jill Boettger, Courtney Thompson and to all the many, many people in the community whose support has made a huge difference to my writing – whether they knew it or not! As always, a special thanks needs to go out to everyone from my days on the *filling Station* collective, and especially to Doug Steedman, Russ Rickey, Tom Muir, Jacqueline Turner and Rajinderpal S. Pal, whose examples continue to guide my own work.

IAN SAMUELS is a former editor of *filling Station* magazine and currently works at WordFest: Banff-Calgary International Writers Festival. He is the author of one previous collection of poetry titled *Cabra* (Red Deer Press, 2000). He lives in his hometown of Calgary, where he is currently working on a mythic history of once-famous blues venue the King Edward hotel.